Elizabeth Blackwell

A LIFE OF DILIGENCE

by Ann-Marie Kishel

Lerner Publications Company • Minneapolis

Photo Acknowledgments

The images in this book are used with the permission of: The Schlesinger Library, Radcliffe Institute, Harvard University, pp. 4, 19; © Getty Images, p. 6; The Granger Collection, New York, pp. 7, 20; North Wind Picture Archives, pp. 8, 10, 12, 16; Library of Congress, pp. 11 (LC-DIG-ppmsca-11773), 24 (LC-USZ62-2053), 26 (LC-USZ62-57850); Archives and Special Collections on Women in Medicine, Drexel University College of Medicine, pp. 13, 23 (both); The Art Archive/Culver Pictures, p. 14; Courtesy The National Library of Medicine, pp. 17, 18, 25; The Art Archive/J Clarence Davies coll/Museum of the City of New York/29.100.2310, p. 22. Front Cover: © Bettmann/CORBIS.

Lerner Publications Company
A division of Lerner Publishing Group
241 First Avenue North
Minneapolis, MN 55401 U.S.A.

Website address: www.lernerbooks.com

Words in **bold type** are explained in a glossary on page 31.

Library of Congress Cataloging-in-Publication Data

Kishel, Ann-Marie.
    Elizabeth Blackwell : a life of diligence / by Ann-Marie Kishel.
      p. cm. – (Pull ahead books)
    Includes index.
    ISBN-13: 978-0-8225-6459-1 (lib. bdg. : alk. paper)
    ISBN-10: 0-8225-6459-9 (lib. bdg. : alk. paper)
    1. Blackwell, Elizabeth, 1821–1910–Juvenile literature. 2. Women physicians–New York (State)–Biography–Juvenile literature. 3. Women physicians–England–Biography–Juvenile literature. I. Title.
R154.B623K55 2007
610.92–dc22
                                                 2006021943

Manufactured in the United States of America
1 2 3 4 5 6 – JR – 12 11 10 09 08 07

Table of Contents

Elizabeth Blackwell

Growing Up

Have you ever worked really hard for something you wanted? Elizabeth Blackwell was a hard worker. She knew what she wanted. She found a way to do it. Her **diligence** made her the first American woman to go to **medical school** and become a doctor.

Elizabeth was born in the city of Bristol.

Elizabeth was born in Great Britain in 1821. Her family moved to the United States when she was eleven years old. Her father died six years later.

Elizabeth's family did not have much money. Elizabeth needed to work. She became a teacher.

Elizabeth was a teacher like this woman.

A doctor gives a check-up to a sick child.

Another Idea

Elizabeth did not like teaching, but women did not have many job choices then. A friend told Elizabeth she would be a good doctor. Elizabeth knew it would be difficult to become a doctor. She also knew that sick women would be more comfortable with a **female** doctor.

Women often cared for sick people. But at this time, they were not allowed to be doctors.

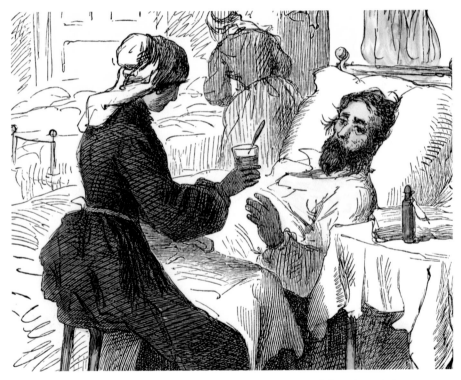

Many women became nurses and cared for the sick.

Like these women, Elizabeth decided to go to college.

Elizabeth decided to become a doctor. She continued to work as a teacher to earn money to pay for medical school.

Only men were allowed at medical school.

Many medical schools would not accept her. They did not want female students.

Finally a school said yes! Elizabeth was very happy. Her diligence started to pay off.

Elizabeth studied at Geneva Medical College in New York.

Elizabeth and other students watch an operation.

Medical School

Elizabeth was the first woman in the United States to go to medical school. She was a good student. She studied hard. She finished first in her class. Elizabeth still needed to practice what she had learned.

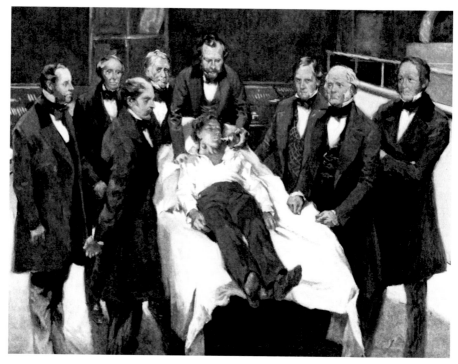
Most hospitals only hired men as doctors.

Elizabeth had a hard time finding a job. No one wanted to **hire** a woman. But she kept looking.

Eventually she found work at **hospitals** in France and then Great Britain. She worked very hard.

Elizabeth worked at this hospital in Paris, France.

Elizabeth returned to the United States. She wanted to open her own doctor's office.

The doctor's office that Elizabeth wanted might have looked like this one.

Elizabeth had trouble finding an office.

Some building owners would not rent her a place for an office. They did not think a woman should be a doctor. Elizabeth kept looking.

20

Dr. Blackwell

At last, Elizabeth found a building for her office. At first, she did not have many **patients**. So Elizabeth wrote speeches about healthy living. She spoke to groups of people in church basements. They learned about her work. This helped her get more patients.

Elizabeth opened a **clinic** for poor people in New York City. Soon she had many patients.

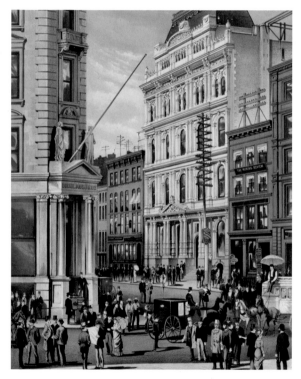

Elizabeth opened her first clinic in New York City.

Elizabeth's sister, Dr. Emily Blackwell *(left)*, and Dr. Marie Zakrzewska *(right)* worked at Elizabeth's clinic.

Elizabeth's sister also became a doctor. She worked with Elizabeth at her clinic. Another female doctor worked with them too.

Women attend a class at Elizabeth's medical school.

Together the three doctors opened a small hospital in New York City. Later, they started a medical school for women.

Elizabeth moved to Great Britain. She worked to start another medical school for women.

Elizabeth also started the London School of Medicine for Women.

A Life of Diligence

Elizabeth worked hard and helped people her whole life. She knew that she wanted to be a doctor. She wanted other women to be able to become doctors too. Her diligence helped her to achieve her goals.

ELIZABETH BLACKWELL TIMELINE

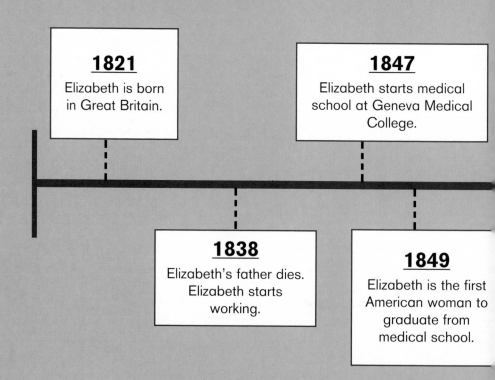

1821
Elizabeth is born in Great Britain.

1847
Elizabeth starts medical school at Geneva Medical College.

1838
Elizabeth's father dies. Elizabeth starts working.

1849
Elizabeth is the first American woman to graduate from medical school.

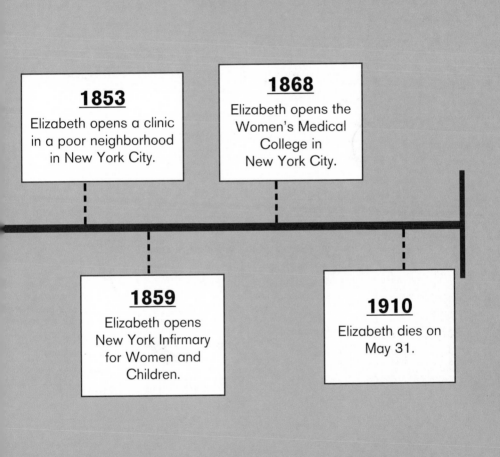

More about
Elizabeth Blackwell

● Elizabeth adopted her daughter, Katherine Barry, in 1854.

● Elizabeth trained nurses to care for injured soldiers during the Civil War, 1861–1865.

● Elizabeth was pictured on a U.S. postage stamp in 1973.

Websites

Hobart and William Smith Colleges: Elizabeth Blackwell, M.D.
http://campus.hws.edu/his/blackwell

Library of Congress: Elizabeth Blackwell Graduates
http://www.americaslibrary.gov/cgi-bin/page.cgi/jb/reform/blackwell_1

National Library of Medicine: Elizabeth Blackwell
http://www.nlm.nih.gov/hmd/blackwell

Glossary

clinic: a place where sick people go to talk to a doctor

diligence: working hard to get something done

female: a girl or woman

hire: to give someone a job

hospitals: places where sick people go to get well

medical school: a school where people study to become doctors

patients: sick people who are seeing a doctor to get better

Index